Deep in the valley

Bobbi Bisset

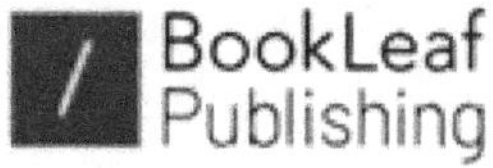

Presentation by *BookLeaf Publishing*

Web: www.bookleafpub.com

E-mail: info@bookleafpub.com

ISBN: 9789357210348

First edition 2022

DEDICATION

To anyone who could be in the valley, at any point and feels unsure of the way out.

One step at a time, always forward and never back.

ACKNOWLEDGEMENT

Frankie, my one and only.
To my children and family.
"Ste" from Rite Flank support group.
"Jess" the vegan - my doppelganger
Every therapist who has ever helped me.
Anti-depressants.
My internal love for myself and feeling worth
keeping around.

PREFACE

True email sent to a friend:

Hi Ste, hope you and your family are well.

I wanted to email and say that I saw you and your family a few weeks ago shopping in Aldi. I didn't let on and felt like shit after.

So here's why:
Exactly 8 weeks ago I was planning on killing myself. I had every intention as I felt there was no way out. Feels like a shitty thing to say 8 weeks later. Someone said "oh it will ease", another said "you just feel hopeless, you don't mean it".
People mean well but they know nothing about being at the bottom of the pit. I am female (suggested maybe a hormonal one!), I have a good job, wonderful friends and family; lots of reasons to not be at the bottom of the pit!

By some divine intervention I didn't harm myself 8 weeks ago. I wanted to tell you that, regardless of how much good advice and love people close to me showed, it was your content that swayed my decision. Feel pretty ashamed to

not say my family but it is the truth. I have seen
the impact of loss (of which you and so many)
have had and it kept me clinging to the tiny light
above the pit. I wanted you to know this value
and appreciation.

Back when I saw you in Aldi, I wasn't brave
enough to let on as I was scared of bursting into
tears, just so you understand.

Keep up your hard work and inspiration, for men
and women, all who may one day be at the
bottom of the pit.

Deep in the valley

My depression is out of hand.
My depression is winning the battle.
My naughty cheerleaders called insecurity and gloom are loud in my ears.
I'm fucking sick of hearing "cheer up" or "turn that frown upside down".
What I need is a way to rid my mind of my depression and my shitty cheerleaders.
Radio silence is the aim and that has nothing to do with smiling.
No one gets how I feel.
Some people appear to have their own black depression dog or are lucky enough to only have temporary visits.
My dog is constantly there and is howling in my ears.
It's like the dog is in pain and then inflicts the pain onto me.
My husband looks at me, like, what now. What is she crying about?
Can you not see the fucking dog? Or hear the howling?
He blankly stares back, confused and not understanding any of it.
He has no dog and never has.

He has no naughty cheerleaders.
He has no battle to fight.

My name is Misery

"You are miserable to fuck all the time".
Sorry to inconvenience you with my sad face,
my true feelings coming to the surface.
Sorry that I am not "Miss Sunshine", shit and
giggles.
Sorry that I lack emotion or give a toot about
much - it is better than feeling everything all at
once.
FYI I'm not miserable to fuck, I'm lost, in the
darkness of depression - without a map out of
the sadness.
Someone please turn on the light.

Is it a pit or is it a valley?

Living in the darkness is one of the worst
feelings.
I stumble around trying to make sense of the
world but I do not see anything clearly.
I cry an awful lot and feel permanently sorry for
myself.
The numbness has started to ease and now pity
has taken over.
I have empathy fatigue for others too - which is
completely out of character.
I don't have much to say to anyone.
I speak to myself all day, in my head, so I am
too exhausted.
I look around for daylight to break - above the
valley that I am in.
I fear I am not in a valley this time.
I have a sense that I am in a dark, wet, cold pit.
How on earth did this happen, how did I get here
and what has changed this time?
Is there any light above the pit then?
I start to wail, confused and lost.
I need to find a way out.

Help

Ring ring, ring ring.

"Hello?"

"Hello, this is your doctors surgery, we have a letter here from, erm, October time that says that you may require a medication review. Do you still need this?"

My brain is shocked.

My plans are all frozen.

I see a tiny bit of light above my pit.

I asked for help months ago and out of the blue I get this call.

My mind tries to be stubborn and convince me to say I am fine.

I take a breath and think back to the feelings I have had for months, all leading me to this sadness.

"Yes please - I am still struggling".

"The Doctor will call you on the Public holiday if that's okay."

Further shock descends - is this divine intervention?

When do you ever get a call back from a doctor and get an appointment 4 days later on a public holiday?

Regardless, I am grateful and the light has
started to peek out at me and give me a new
found hope.
I will accept the help.

Turning on the light

Turning on the light takes a huge amount of
strength.
Asking for help in any form feels impossible;
when you feel unworthy.
Doctor talked about admitting me - wait what?
That suggestion struck fear into me, am I that
unwell?
I refuse admittance. I accept medication instead.
I am waiting for cognitive behaviour therapy.
Doctor agrees a safety plan - this must be
serious.
I feel slightly relieved, my hope clinging on to a
tiny bit of self worth.
I make a list:
2022 -
Take medication forever.
Use the gym.
Love your family.
Stop eating crap.
Clear out the demons.

Grief

Grief is sneaky.
Little angry ninjas bouncing around your head.
Kicking your brain, until the tears overflow out
of your eyes.
Your heart aches exactly like the day you were
left behind in the real world.
You feel dazed and wonder what sparked the
feelings.
The ninjas retreat but they can descend at any
time.
They hide in the darkness, waiting for weakness.

It is all around us.

Sadness fills the room as I walk into it.
I feel I am radiated sadness, despite my false smile.
I cannot hold eye contact.
I fear someone will see into my dark soul and depression.
The lady announces "Welcome everyone to the well being class".
My sadness lifts; it is hard to believe all these smiling people have dark souls or sadness like I do.
Depression is everywhere, we just don't notice it enough.
Eye contact may have alerted me sooner.

End game?

"What is the end game to writing a book?"
Reasonable innocent question, which makes me feel
silly, hurt and a little bit embarrassed.
I'm a little lost for words - I cannot justify myself
without feeling angry.
My (lack of) confidence is screaming in my ears to be
quiet and hide my truth from everyone.
I took a breath - a deep one and said;
The end game is feeling worthy of something
(anything)
The end game is showing others they are not alone
and that we all have complex minds.
The end game is to save my own life; a reminder to
never get into these lands again.

Boiling point

Some people are rude,
so many are inconsiderate.
It is no wonder peoples' confidence can shatter
so easily.
A simple smile, acknowledgement or gesture is
all that is needed.
Interrupting my chat today has triggered my
anger.
How dare you draw someone away from a chat
so rudely.
Waving your arms, making a "pssssttt" noise
from afar and indicating to move next door.
My temper is back, my feelings are raw.
My patience has deserted me but there is no real
excuse for being rude.
Once alone I am left feeling foolish and
flustered.
Boiling point is an unpleasant and easy place to
be at the moment

Reactive

I have gone from one extreme and another
Silence and feeling very little,
to rage and opinionated.
I feel like I cannot get a happy medium - I am all
or nothing.
This makes me sad and anxious.
I feel hurt by everyone at the moment,
I can see when they take me for granted or are
rude to me.
It feels excessively unacceptable and it is
triggering something deep inside me.
Should I have more tolerance for idiots?
When I reflect on how I ended in this place,
lots of my issues come down to disgraceful
encounters in my past.
Times need to change - reactive is not suited to
me, nor is silence.
I need to think of myself as the caterpillar that
needs to grow into a butterfly.

Therapy

The lady in therapy has a kind face.
The lady looked fearful at hearing my worst
story,
from my childhood.
She asked me to stop talking and encouraged me
to breathe.
Inhale for 4 seconds, hold for 4 seconds and
exhale for 4 more seconds.
I didn't realise but I must take one breath,
and spit out my humiliating story without
breathing properly.
I start crying like I am 8 years old again.
I close my eyes and see my bright blonde hair,
wearing a red t-shirt and smiling from ear to ear.
I remembered feeling so conflicted and sad at
such a young age.
I did not think I was ever pretty or attractive in
any way.
I used to lie, compulsively to avoid anyone
finding out the truth in my eyes.
I was frightened all the time and I think this has
ruined my brain.
I opened my eyes and looked back at the
therapist -
she could clearly see my face was sad.

"Tell me what you were thinking?"
I have wasted my life feeling ashamed.

The flower between the thorns

Four strangers on a table.
One female and three men.
Men look terrified that they may offend.
Female is feeling humiliated for gate crashing
the males table.
Awkward talk - about the weather, football and
cars takes place.
Female is lipreading as she cannot hear.
The men do not appear to notice but will close
down further if they are told.
The men are attending today for physio support -
the female for mental health.
The men sternly drink out of their coffee cups
and shut that topic down.
No one really knows how to deal with complex
minds,
but closing down creates paranoia and red
cheeks.
The men all appear so controlled and average
but the female feels otherwise.
In a flush the female orders the wrong food and
realises she looks stupid.
Human nature clicked and the humans all started
laughing and teasing one another.

The ice was broken.
Everyone looked settled and happier.
It was clear that while some cannot talk about
certain topics,
nice humans can communicate warmth in so
many other ways.
By nature females are generally more emotional,
while men can be aloof - neither are wrong.
We decide how long we want to be a thorn or a
flower.

Trauma doppelganger

I met someone who has a cutting story like my
own.
We both said things that seemed to stick to the
other person,
both knowing the feelings and meanings.
I saw sadness in her eyes that I often feel in my
own when I describe my story.
Children should always be believed - always.
Children should always have one safe parent -
always.
Without these two things,
me and my trauma doppelganger feel lost in this
big world.
Alone without a map around our emotions and
relationships.
Too scared to upset the apple cart,
unless it is our own damaged and devastated
apple cart.
I have a sense of relief.
Hopeful that I can be as wonderful as my
doppelganger;
who's eyes dance with knowledge and hope.
I hope I can bring her comfort too.
We may be without a positive parent,
But we both believe one another.

Inner critic

I feel like I am regaining some of my old self.
Confidence seems to have abandoned me lately.
It is a nice warm feeling when someone tells me
I smell nice.
I feel flush to my cheeks and cannot form a
response.
I feel confused that I may appeal to the public.
My inner critic screams - smells of what?
I am learning to cast aside this inner voice and
make it hush up.
It does not matter what I smell of; my inner
critic is missing the point.

I should have been a cave woman.

Loneliness should not have any place in today's world.

Most people have phones, social media, music, hustle and bustle nearby.

Even so, the busiest of lives can feel very isolated.

As humans we need to focus on what gives us emotional warmth.

Laughing with friends, smile from others or doing something we enjoy.

This is what we need more of.

No fancy cars, designer trainers and jobs that suck.

Cavemen didn't have any modern day advances.

Cavemen were probably very rested, happy and smiley people.

They clearly had a different sort of threat, but personally I'd prefer a dinosaur over prolonged loneliness.

Spring clean

I have a closet full of skeletons which no one
really knows about.
Each one reminds me daily of my failures in the
past.
Some are huge and disgusting, some are not so
bad,
all of them make me embarrassed, sad or mad.
So I have decided to pull them out.
One by one I am dusting them down and asking
them to stay away.
I am dragging them to an open grave,
a place far away.
Each one will be thrown deep inside,
with little chance to find me again.
My skeletons must be tired too,
Sick of calling my name.

Apology to myself

Dear little girl self, teenage self and adult self.
I am sorry for not believing in you for a long
time.
I see now that you were mistreated by people
you loved,
and this broke your spirit.
You are beautiful, clever, thoughtful and very
wise.
You work hard to help others so they do not get
their spirits damaged too.
I wish I could take away the pain and erase the
bad times -
however a strong personality is born out of
challenging times.
I will not let myself down ever again - I will get
the treatment I need and sustain changes.
I am proud of myself, my battle scars, warts and
all.
My inner child does not need to be scared
anymore,
I am a grown up woman now, ready for less
talking and more action.
I see you, I love you, I need you all.

Recovery

At last,
my recovery has started.
It seems to have dragged me kicking and
screaming through the darkest of days.
I do feel that I am full of hope, compassion and
love for myself.
This is unlike my previous self.
I am going to take a day at a time, practise as I
preach, say "no" more often and love my
existence every.single.day.
I am proud of myself for turning the lights on,
accepting help
and making good progress.
I have some way to go and I will not pretend it
has been easy.
I am still somewhat in the valley, out of the pit
and heading towards the summit.
Life is good and gracious.
Love yourself first and then everyone else.

People in the pit.

If any of these words resonate
and you feel inside your own head, pit or valley;
then I urge anyone to seek help.

Google help.
Call a crisis number.
Speak to a friend.
Call the Police.

You are worth a million stars.
People will shed tears in your absence.
You are needed and wanted somewhere.

Medication.
Therapy.
Talking.
Quit your job.
Stopping bad habits.

Identify your demon and slay it.
Then live life as the person,
who escaped the valley of depression.

www.ingramcontent.com/pod-product-compliance
Lightning Source LLC
LaVergne TN
LVHW021719210726
843509LV00021B/2594